Six Poems and a Song

Bruce McCandless III

ISBN-13: 9780998335100
ISBN-10: 099833510X
Library of Congress Control Number: 2016918413
Ninth Planet Press, Austin, TX

Oro en Paz, Fierro en Guerra

Acknowledgments

Portions of "A Beginner's Guide to Disappointment" previously appeared in *Nebo* and *Proposing on the Brooklyn Bridge*. "Foot Soldiers" was originally published in *Borderlands*. "The All-Time Traveling Haiku All-Stars" was originally published in *Cold Mountain Review*, and "Baz" first appeared in *Asphodel*. The author thanks the editors of these journals and anthologies for permission to reprint these poems.

Many thanks go also to Bernice McCandless, Bruce McCandless II, Pati McCandless, Jeanette Scott, David Weiser, Gayle Gordon, Mark Robbins, and Roger G. Worthington for their help and patience with this project.

Acknowledgments

Table of Contents

Six Poems and a Song

The Japanese attack on Pearl Harbor commenced a little before eight a.m. on a Sunday morning. It involved three hundred sixty-six airplanes, which dropped several thousand tons of explosives on the American ships at anchor. Twenty-four hundred and three Americans were killed in the attack; another eleven hundred and seventy-eight were wounded. The Empire of Japan declared war on the United States shortly afterward.

Harpies were winged creatures of Greek and Roman mythology, monstrous in aspect and associated with the spirits of the winds.

The Turning Point

1. Attack

Hawaii. December 7, 1941.

They came out of the clouds at dawn
like harpies from the halls of night,
cruel heralds of a distant emperor
spurring steel-spined warbirds through the sky.
With ghosts of gods and sacred ancestors
these men brought death to the idle round-eyes.
Their guns spat lead, raked runways
for flesh and machine, and on long dives
the planes dropped metal fish to crack the keels
of ships that stood anchored for provisioning.
The Yankee wings were destroyed
on the ground where they lay—86ed—kiboshed—
their crews cut in two by the guns,
engulfed as they fled by flowers of flame.
Arizona shuddered and broke
in the harbor, back buckled by fire, and
many men fell in the chaos of that attack—
littered the fuel-soaked asphalt of the airfield or
floated like petals of some bitter bloom
on the harbor's smoke-choked waters.

As the assassins escaped across
the whale realm in their warbirds,
relieved by the ruin of the stunned Republic,
at home on green islands the enemy rejoiced to hear tales
of Yankees slain and their sea homes sent to shark fields,

"Chrysanthemum Throne" refers to both a real throne, located in Kyoto, and, as synecdoche, to the institution of the Japanese monarchy, which can be traced back some twenty-five hundred years.

The state religion of Japan was (and is) Shintoism, which recognizes the emperor as a descendant of gods, and therefore partly divine. Amaterasu is a sun goddess, and a major deity in the Shinto pantheon.

the bone orchards beneath the wave road.
And on the hidden Chrysanthemum Throne
where the Emperor God communed
with the spirits of his forebears in
unbroken line back to the sun goddess herself
(*Amaterasu*; Light That Walked on Earth),
it seemed clear the blessings of history had been given
and rightly bestowed, as the island empire's eastern threat
lay charred and headless in dead sea port Pearl.
The war was over. As good as done.

2. Invocation

Belt it out American muses,
demigods of Denver, Dubois, and Detroit—
you the Bakersfield rodeo sweetheart,
wheat-field blonde on the sun-warped bleachers;
you, the almond-eyed Syrian's daughter
alone in a doorway beneath doom lights of Rahway,
dismal jewelry of the Jersey night;
you, washerwoman of Memphis,
pouring soft cocktails of syrup and sarcasm
in Jim Crow memories of Mississippi
and you, teen princess of the Texas truck stop,
your cheekbones monuments to proud
Cherokee blood, gazing up at
freight trains inching on steel roads through
two-light towns in prehistoric Piney Woods
where men sit vague in lonely hoods of smoke
and sip cups of cooling midnight—
Sing, muses! All states, sing
of fighting on far southern seas,
wherein the Republic—disorganized, ill-disciplined,
country of a thousand thick-armed accents—
was first bloodied by the Empire of the Rising Sun,
and, still reeling, stumbled gun to gun
into the enemy's unthinkable battleship,
gray city of malice and dismembering fire.

The red fuse flares and splits the dark. And so
the wreckage begins. Enough with this prelude.
By the time the klaxons sound, it is already too late.
Our hero wakes. Now show him his fate.

Located on the southeast coast of the island of Oahu, Hanauma Bay is a marine embayment formed by a tuff ring. It remains a popular destination for swimming, snorkeling, and sunbathing. Green sea turtles frequent these waters.

The smoke that rose from Pearl Harbor was caused primarily by burning fuel oil, chiefly Bunker-C type, a high-viscosity residual oil.

Slang expression of surprise or disbelief popular in the 1930s and 40s, often associated with Chicago Cubs baseball announcer Harry Caray.

3. Smoke

In a rental house overlooking the harbor
Sunday stillness lay like a blanket,
seamed with scents of coffee and jasmine.
From her kitchen window, Sue Parrish saw a curious sight.
She woke her husband. (A difficult task.)
Smoke? he said. *No need to worry, as long as it's white.*
Sue gazed down at the resting figure, examined her hands.
Their children slept across the hall: Connor, four, and Mia, two,
fair-haired like their father, born with his sometime-squint.
There had been talk of an outing, a picnic today
to talk to the turtles at Hanauma Bay.
Daughter of a Navy man herself, Sue knew well
the solitary nights and aching long not-knowing of
Pacific cruises, of sudden deployment
to the ends of the world and wondering the worst.
Look at her now: she does not want to say the words
that will send her young lieutenant out the door
into that vast blue haze of letters and imagining.
She says them anyway. *Black as pitch. A lot of it.*
Andy Parrish rises to see for himself the storm clouds bloom
like mushrooms over Pearl, hears the distant dull
thumps as bombs unmake their targets.
Holy Cow! he says. *We're in a fight.*
And then of course the pants and socks,
the breakfast declined because there isn't time,
the Packard coughing as it rounds the bend.

Long after Andy's out of sight,
Sue stands wreathed in surging siren wails,
her brown eyes dark with cement dread,
one arm raised to wave farewell.

Franklin Delano Roosevelt contracted polio, known at the time as "infantile paralysis," in 1921, when he was thirty-nine years old. It left him a paraplegic.

4. The Weeping

News of the disaster darted east by telegraph,
pulses of anger and grief and bleak disbelief,
and in Chicago saloons the men of the meat yards
as in plank-board churches Kansas farmers
and in union halls house carpenters of South Dakota
huddled brow-to-brow to share their woe.
In Minnesota and Wisconsin proud workers
of Norwegian stock, once the northern ocean's owners,
set down their hammers and their hand drills,
their scythes and rakes and socket wrenches,
and dreamt black dreams of quick defeat.
Proud and chaotic in a thousand kitchens
women wailed to hear of menfolk vanquished
with no chance even to unlimber guns,
their sky splitters, their metal piercers,
as red-sunned warbirds drove their daggers deep.
Nor were the hellish headlines only of American woe:
Hong Kong, Malaya, and Siam all
felt the bright blade's bite, and sent urgent pleas for aid.
Thus were Japan's ambitions revealed:
a sphere of slaves sustained by terror,
constrained to serve the Emperor God, and
a thousand men sent daily down to dark.

Within the walls of his white palace
the Republic's chair-bound leader, a clever man, and fierce,
sat stunned by word of the attack as
aides and attaches filed in, ashen with the wicked news.
Brave were the words and stern the vows
of the Crippled King as he thought then of

President Roosevelt spoke to Congress on December 8, 1941. The United States declared war on Japan later that day.

his countrymen struck down, of a nation shamed
and slow to anger, but trembling now in mounting wrath.
He took to radio, its electric waves a web around the world,
and defied the Empire—called it out—railed against
the perfidy of its dawn attack on a day
all men knew to be America's time of worship.
He bade the nation assemble, and so it did, in solemn circles
around Marconi's machine, as the Crippled King
exhorted each state's senators. This, he said, is a
date that will live as long as shame exists:
a black day; a treacherous day, as dark as the oil
streaming from shredded hulls in Hawaii's harbor.
Summoning the strength of every warlike god that ruled
the Broad Land's citizens in former times, he called down upon
the Empire horrors of revenge and retribution:
bone for bone; blood for blood—
a storm of righteous fire and coiled rage.

As it was widely feared that the Japanese would attempt to invade Hawaii, many military families were evacuated soon after the attack on Pearl Harbor.

5. Bewildered

Andy Parrish worked each day in port
till he could work no more, then
fell down hatchways to grab some shut-eye,
emerging hours later to hoist a cup
of jitter juice and take up tasks anew.
His ship, the *San Francisco*, was little damaged in the attack,
so her mariners pitched in to refit others
as all prepared to take the wave roads west to war.
By the time the young lieutenant departed Pearl
on Christmas Day of '41,
Sue and the kids were sailing home at eighteen knots
on steam liner *Lurline*, pride of the Matson fleet,
but stripped now of pretension—bereft of all her finery—
a living room for Yankee wives and frightened tots.
Through winter seas they steamed toward the Golden Gate,
haunted by rumor and a thousand spectral sightings:
the outlines of aircraft in an oystery sky,
the stalk of a submarine scope to starboard,
glimpsed for a moment through wind-tossed waves.
Sue carried flatware, life insurance policies, and
a medical kit she'd bought for the boy, his only Yuletide gift.
The three of them ate powdered eggs off paper plates and
lived in fear of the next bad news.
For some, their menfolk slept
in pine boxes in the cargo hold,
felled by the sudden spear thrust from Japan.
Sue wrote letters on the backs of envelopes, wondering
if she could hold her children if the ship went down,
or worse, could hold only the *one*;
wondering where her husband was,
dreading what the braiders of the future had in store
for an injured people, stunned by all it saw.

In contemporary slang, a "palooka" was a journeyman boxer, a "ham-and-egger" noteworthy more for his ability to absorb punishment than for his prowess in the ring.

The Japanese were notoriously cruel to prisoners of war. The Bataan Death March resulted in the deaths of somewhere between six and ten thousand American and Filipino soldiers.

6. Bataan

April 1942.

Just as the palooka, sucker-punched and pawing air,
fights to pull himself up off the floor,
so the Republic scrambled to
collect its forces, wary of death blows still to come.
Daily the Emperor's army advanced; across the sea
Burma, Hong Kong, and Singapore fell
before the Rising Sun, bent the knee to the conqueror's sword.
In the Philippines' jade jungle ravines
General Wainright's GIs, outflanked by Japanese forces,
gave up their weapons and were enslaved.
Their captors marched them miles through heat and hills
to camps where they would spend the war.
Along the way those who were too sick to walk
were beaten, starved, run over by trucks where they lay in the mud,
had their heads cut off to rot in the sun.
How many Yanks and Filipinos died along
that trail of tears cannot be told,
as no white or brown man's death
was deemed important enough to be recorded,
but the human chaff of those grim weeks lies
to this day beneath the leaves of Bataan,
seeds of the Empire's planned prosperity,
spores of black buds slow to bloom.

United States Marine Corps, First Division—sometimes known as the "Old Breed." Based at Camp Pendleton, near San Diego.

Thermopylae, or the "hot gates," is the site where a band of Greek warriors, led by three hundred Spartans, held off a much larger Persian imperial invasion force in 480 B.C. The name refers to hot springs in the area. It was said to be the gate to hell.

While emphasizing the divine spark resident in the human soul, the Judeo-Christian tradition has long resisted the notion that a man may himself be divine, with the notable exception among Christians of Jesus.

7. An Unimportant Island

August 1942.

Dark days now.
The gall of losses, and long rolls of the dead.
The enemy advancing everywhere. It was only
through subterfuge and sheerest chance
the 1st Marines took a piece of
a sea dot in the Solomons called Guadalcanal—
mosquito-massed, choked with snake-vine—
and soon began to bleed. The Emperor's men
came nightly shrieking through the jungle,
vowing death to the mongrel Republic
for the impertinence of standing up
against the gods and the gods' pure warrior race.
Just as at the Hot Gates the Persian sent forth his
legions to crash against the swords of the Spartans,
so now did the Japanese general send his men to win or die.
The leathernecks dug deep in mud as
doom crashed down upon them:
infantry onslaughts, skin rippers dropped from the sky,
long-range shells lobbed in from floating fortresses offshore.
Under-provisioned, gasping with fever,
these men had no regard for self-proclaimed divinity!
They were hard guys mostly, knuckleheads and average joes,
garish in their prominent clavicles.
They were Utah boys, raised on incredible sunlight,
and sons of Polock Ohio and the massive foundries there
that sipped from holy Cuyahoga; also fast-talking Bronx men,
angel-headed hipsters burning for the ancient heavenly connection
to the starry dynamo in the machinery of night,

Atabrine, a trade name for a preparation of quinocrine hydrochloride, was dispensed in tablet form to American military men in the South Pacific to combat malaria.

General Alexander Archer Vandegrift (1887-1973).

The Marines dug and lived in shallow excavations that provided some protection from artillery strikes and aerial bombardment.

desperate for a coffin nail and a cup of java.
They lived on nicotine and atabrine.
They were stubborn, restless, unwilling to die
but too proud to be dislodged.
The Marine commander, Vandegrift, ordered all to hold the line,
and so they did, slack-jawed, subterranean,
crawling out only when the fire storm ceased
and the screams came quickly toward them again:

MARINE, YOU DIE!

Then the machine gun chattered
its mechanical aria, barrel sizzling in the rain,
and the Emperor's men went to meet their silent ancestors
in dim worlds where no time piece runs.

The Italian inventor and electrical engineer Guglielmo Marconi is widely considered to be the father of radio, or "wireless telegraphy," as it was sometimes called.

"Magic" was the cryptograph assigned to the U.S. effort to break Japan's system of coded communications, which was itself assigned the names Red, Blue, and, finally, at the time of Pearl Harbor, Purple. Purple was a code system enhanced by Nazi Germany's assistance.

Henderson Field was the American air base on Guadalcanal.

The U.S.S. O'Bannon was a Fletcher-class destroyer named after Marine Lieutenant Presley O'Bannon, who led a contingent of Marines in their dramatic assault on the Libyan city of Derna in 1805.

8. Arsenal of the Underworld

November 1942.

But how long could Thermopylae hold?
Through long red weeks of war
the leathernecks grew tired, gaunt, racked with disease.
The Imperial Army strengthened its forces weekly,
determined to push the Republic's defenders off
the strip of jungle mud they bled to keep.
Rising Sun ships churned the straits off Guadalcanal,
bringing guns and munitions and ever more warriors
to drive the mongrels from their seaside hold.
What use this island was outside the scope of war cannot be told.
It was no place wise men desired.
Yet somehow now the world turned toward
this dismal stage as enemies locked in mortal strife
came quick to pit against each other all their desperate strength.
The Emperor required it to guard his newly minted
slaveholds, and his minions determined to make it so.
These votaries crouched around their Marconi machines,
sent out sound waves through the skies,
enchanted to the sound of nonsense,
but in basements back at Pearl thin men sat listening,
making magic of their own to reassemble scrambled sounds,
to crawl into the heads of empire.
And when in bleak long corridors of November
the Japanese steamed down to bombard the warbirds
at Henderson Field, an American counter-force was sent to stop them:
Atlanta, Juneau, Portland—proud frigates of proud cities—
and destroyers bearing names of the Broad Land's heroes
of brighter days: *O'Bannon, Stennet,* and *Aaron Ward.*
All told the makeshift armada was thirteen ships—
six thousand swabs sent out to turn the tide of war.

Among the massed gray hulls was *San Francisco*,
Parrish's ship, and Andy stood
his watch on the signal bridge,
staring into corners of that coming midnight
as if he might never see another.

The Yankee floating fortresses advanced in file
beneath a moonless, flower-scented southern sky,
searching for an enemy in those treacherous seas,
probing with electronic fingers far into shadow,
alert for monsters in the mist.

9. A Letter from Long Beach

Sue's latest letter brought encouragement,
news of Connor and Mia and far-flung cousins, of towels purchased
for a pretty price and sure to wear for ages.
So the War Department urged:
Short and cheerful! Or we'll censor!
Just a note to let them know you care!
She was living with her folks in Long Beach.
The kids were making pals, and truly all was swell at home.
But stowed among the lines as well
were words of longing, tinted purple,
reminiscences of things they'd sworn to do
before the tide of war swept all to destinations unforeseen,
fly-specks on some faded map of dread and sour midnights.
And sometimes in the fading light of evening
Sue walked along the Pacific shore, one eye
on her children, busy at their play,
but her mind in meantime roaming
far to sea, searching for her husband
who rode steam turbines
further forward toward that place at last
where aspiration meets the actual,
and fate sorts future from the past.

Radar, a word derived from the phrase "radio detection and ranging," was developed concurrently by the British and several other nations in the years before World War II. Radar units were attached to some American ships early in 1942.

A sea monster referenced in the Tanakh, or Old Testament, the name "Leviathan" has become synonymous with any large aquatic animal. In the 19th Century, it was a common appellation for the whale. One such creature sank the whaling ship Essex in 1820, and served as a model for the elusive white whale pursued by Ahab in Moby-Dick.

10. Encounter

November 12, 1942.

The American admiral was Daniel Callaghan,
a long-time salt enamored of old ways of war.
He did not take kindly to the new machines,
these radar devices and their ungainly antennae
bolted to the superstructures of his ships.
He led his column of high metal masts through blackness,
trusting in the captains of his foremost craft to know the night.
As he steamed his force of thirteen ships due north
his mariners knew well, from captain down to cook's mate,
what waited for them in those straits:
to test the Empire's battle group was likely suicide.
Callaghan shared little. Perhaps he was
perplexed himself about how to halt a convoy
that could outgun his gray ships two-to-one.
Perhaps he knew and wouldn't say the obvious.
He planned to fight them anyway, despite ill omens,
and drag to death as many as he could.
He placed his radar-mounted masts astern
and listened without speaking as they warned
of enemy contact—of something massive
moving toward them, dead ahead.

Imagine yourself a whaler of old,
a harpoon man, Nantucket-born,
rocking on broad South Sea swells
several hollers from your ship.
Now see Leviathan, colossus of the deep,
eighty feet from brutal head to massive flukes,
come shimmering up toward you
through the gray-green ocean's veil.
The specter rises from the depths like dread—
grows vaster with each second
until fury fills the eye and flashes

Hiei, the "Black Mountain," was named for a peak that is visible from Kyoto, an important Japanese port city. The ship had fifty-two guns, displaced thirty-seven thousand tons, and was capable of a top speed of thirty knots. She sailed with a crew of over thirteen hundred men.

British naval architect George Thurston.

from the sea like an avalanche from underneath,
forty tons of muscle and ill will
now crashing back beside you with a wave
sharp-steep enough to send your flimsy sea craft down.
So the enemy bows slid from the night
like axe blades swung at the Yankee masts.
Whale man, grip your metal mongery—your
single slender iron fang. Mouth a prayer.
And *heave*! What else is there to do?

The gods brought the forces face to face before
they'd properly measured each other;
through pre-dawn's ink they steamed together, keel for keel,
Republic and Imperial Navy intermixed.
The *Hiei* was largest of the dreadnoughts there,
the Emperor's giant among giants, a death ship fully
30,000 tons of steel and steam and diesel oil,
porcupined with massive guns.
She'd been designed by a man of the pleasant islands,
an Old Worlder who little knew the role she'd come to play.
Spotlights like the eyes of monstrous animals
intersected on the formless tide, and for several moments
the disbelieving ocean riders tried to fathom what they saw.
Then—like a dream destroyed by a sudden fall—came the *roar*:
hammering concussive blasts shivering
the metal skin of grim sea cities,
crushing bridges, decks, barbettes and guns.
Like some cavalry charge from a distant century
combatants rushed each other, big barrels spitting death.
The night sky pulsed with scarlet star-shell light
as if the idiot denizens of hell had slipped
the bounds of their infernal prison to trouble earth
and smear the sea with brains and blood.

Among those killed by the Japanese shell were Captain Cassin Young. At Pearl Harbor, Young was blown off the U.S.S. Vestal during the Japanese attack. He swam through oily water to return to his ship, and was able to navigate her to a place of relative safety. He was awarded the Congressional Medal of Honor for his actions.

11. First Blows

Who now can say
what madness opened up upon those waters?
Atlanta was first to feel the enemy's spears.
Spotlighted by *Hiei* with the strength of 50,000 candles,
the Yank steel city stood alone in sudden silhouette.
The *Hiei* spat fire from her 14-inchers,
massive ship-crushing shells screaming
parallel to sea to find their mark in men and metal.
Tracers sped like angry bees toward their targets.
Men were blown off decks into oblivion and
cold ocean poured through punctured ship walls, drowning all below.
The *Frisco* took the fight in tight—so close the Death Ship's massive armor
could not shield her from the cruiser's hits—
until an enemy shell screamed into the *San Francisco*'s bridge
where Callaghan and officers, brave men all,
gathered to read the runes of wind and wave.
That twice-cursed blast killed every man save one.
Silence fell over the scene—a horrid tangle
of books and burning clothing, shredded code keys, scattered maps.
Parrish pulled himself out of the wreckage, hot steel
sown like seeds of some dark vine in his head and back,
life fluid flowing from his skull.

Parrish was born and raised in Endicott, Nebraska. After graduating from high school, he spent two years at the Colorado School of Mines before being admitted, on his third attempt, to the U.S. Naval Academy in Annapolis. Achilles was the greatest of the Greek warriors who fought at Troy. According to legend, he was dipped in the River Styx by his mother, Thetis, shortly after he was born, in an attempt to make him impervious to harm. Unfortunately, Thetis held Achilles by the heel when she immersed him. As a result, his heel, which did not get wet, remained vulnerable.

They say a man concussed by blow of iron or explosive blast
will look upon the faces of his friends in absent wonder,
as the workings of his mind re-piece themselves.
Parrish was no man of metal. Nor was he
enchanted with the stuff in which Achilles was anointed.
He came to the sea from mid-continent mountains,
made his way to the academy of mariners and there,
despite his stature, put on the gloves and fought all comers.
Now he picked himself up from the carnage,
searched for his commanders and found them gone
to meet their maker. The bridge was his.
He did not want it. Could not grasp it.
And still the enemy came on,
destroyers *Asagumo, Amatsukaze,* and *Yudachi,*
quick through the sea road's frothing craters,
long guns pouring pain through rain-thick air.
Several seamen gathered round him, watching
as the young lieutenant wiped his forehead from his fingers.

No shame now in quiet retreat:
their captain dead; the ship in flames.
They waited for orders. And so they came.
Prepare to engage, said Parrish.
We're gonna hit 'em again.

Lt. Commander Herbert Schonland won the Congressional Medal of Honor for his actions that night.

A "Mae West" was a life preserver, named after the famous actress.

12. The Battle

Her metal bulwarks bent and torn
so that the ocean's frigid asphalt tumbled in,
the *Frisco* was left wallowing and hard to steer.
Fires flared in the armory, paint locker, and Battle II.
Below steel decks a man named Schonland fought to keep
the vessel afloat and on her con. And so
with Parrish relaying orders, man by man, and
Schonland directing damage control, the ship fought on.
Parrish spied the enemy's steel cities silhouetted in the night,
huge trees of flame against the horizon,
and drove the *Frisco* back into the fray.
Those on land who saw the distant struggle said
with each flash there was revealed a set of ships
seemingly immobilized in a panoply of hatred
and bent on nothing less than mutual ruin.
Parish could not see this wider stage.
His vision tunneled, and sure the
navigation bridge was perdition plenty.
Severed limbs, spent shell casings, and
bodies, still in helmets and Mae Wests,
lay lifeless on the deck. A siren shrieked.
Water cascaded from the ruptured cooling system
of the forward 1.1-inch quads.
A leatherneck who watched from shore wrote:
The sea seemed a sheet of polished obsidian

on which the warships had been dropped,
bulls-eyed amid concentric circles like the shock waves
that form around a stone thrown in a pond.
Tracers arced enormous orange in difficult skies.
All was light; then all was dark.
All was madness. All was waste.
I did not think to see a single man
return from what took place.

The Grumman TBF "Avenger" was a dive bomber that saw extensive use by U.S. Navy and Marine aviators during the war.

Most of the crew were evacuated from the ship; however, almost two hundred sailors went down with the vessel. The Hiei was the first battleship of the Imperial Japanese Navy to be sunk. Its loss was a major loss to the Empire in both tactical and psychological terms.

13. Aftermath

A lull at last. The guns gone cold.
When heaven's gem lit up the sullen sea
four Yankee hulls were done, their men sent down to darkness,
but *San Francisco* steamed to port, following *Helena*,
with three battered vessels in her train.
The *Hiei* fled north in search of safety,
bleeding plumes of liquid fuel.
Avengers followed like vultures.
From high in cloud lanes Yankee flyboys
painted punctures in the crippled target
and late that day the ship went down, first of the
enemy's death cities to founder, her
brave men bound for bone orchards half-buried in the deep.
What lamentations must have poured forth then from the
Chrysanthemum Throne, and from the lungs of
the Emperor's warrior admirals!
And from the hearts of dark-haired
wives and daughters lamentations too—
and disbelief that the mongrel nation could
sink so proud a vessel of the imperial fleet.
As a child free to roam the fields reels from
the sting of wasp or bee,
so now Tokyo called back its hulls
from further fighting in this place of bitter struggle.
The tide of reinforcements ceased.
On land the leathernecks turned back last Japanese assaults
with Tommy guns and KA-BAR knives
and so the island was released:
one small piece of Slaveland purged,
her jungles wet with rain and blood.

The "jeheemie" was an ingenious mobile apparatus for hoisting disabled vessels, allowing them to be towed while ashore.

14. The Wheel Turns

Make no mistake:
this fight was never won by any hundred heroes
turning stony-eyed to pierce the foe with fire
from machine gun or the forward turret.
The war churned quick through heart-strong men
like a furnace burns Kentucky coal.
No beaten bronze could blunt the bomb blast.
No bearded gods walked light among
the swabs and jarheads, grunts and flyboys
to shelter them from phosphorous shells,
from tracer burst, from depth charge
drooping slowly down through silent halls.
Stout were the wills of those who held the guns,
but remember too the large-armed toil
of those who worked the parts stampers and rivet spitters;
those who shaped strong iron and aluminum,
and delved into the earth's deep places
to bring the nation's dark provender to light of day.
With many a cunning device and leverage maker,
including the wild jeheemie and the steam drop hammer,
children of the Broad Land's many states bought victory
truck by truck, wing by steel-bright wing
with sweat and toil and tears and blood.
And when Andy Parrish's cruiser limped back to her namesake city,
fog-bound giant of the nation's western shore, the ship
returned to a people armed and bent on breaking
Slaveworld and the Emperor's sword.

The name "Iron Bottom Sound" came from the fact that so many ships—some fifty, of the navies of the United States, Japan, Australia, and New Zealand—were sunk in this body of water. American naval ships still maintain silence when cruising in these waters, as a sign of respect for the men and vessels lost there. Scores of downed military aircraft also lie at the bottom of the Sound.

Approximately one hundred and eleven thousand U.S. sailors, Marines, and Army infantrymen died in the Pacific Theater of World War II. Another two hundred and fifty thousand were wounded.

15. Recounting

The fight for Iron Bottom Sound
and for the vined ravines of that accursed island,
Guadalcanal, turned the fortunes of the war.
Ever after, America advanced: through atolls, up black beaches,
across green ridges of a hundred fox-holed sea specks
as at home the foundries hummed and hammers rang
and battle wagons issued forth
to snap the spears of empire.
But at what cost did the winning come?
At long last after years of desperate fear
the death-stained sons of Poughkeepsie and El Paso stood in
gardens of the Emperor God and could not quite
put down their weapons. In cold Korea and lush Vietnam,
in political fights on foreign fields
Washington continued warring,
as if bloodlust, once summoned, could not be stilled.
Not always were the wars with honor.
And yet where men dreamed of remaking the world
in one dull image—ruled by race, or monolithic creed—
the Broad Land turned to face the threat.
Let us therefore offer thanks to
pharmacists and shutterbugs,
fraternity boys and luckless farmers' sons who

never wanted to be warriors, soda jerks turned foot soldiers
who watched their Alabama brothers burn and
lost their legs and shut their eyes and surrendered
innocence in nights of Peleliu and Okinawa mud,
sailors sunk in shark fields scanning skies for hopes of rescue
or crouched in ammunition lockers screaming through the hell of
shellfire as their broad steel cities snapped in two.

They do not want your gratitude.
They want to *live*.
Thank them anyway. It is
the only thing you have to give.

The "honky-tonk," or "honk-a-tonk," is an establishment, typically southern or southwestern, that serves alcoholic beverages and provides live or recorded music for patrons. It is sometimes known in the north as a "roadhouse."

16. Return

Andy Parrish lived to steam out of the sun
into broad blue waters of the Frisco Bay,
as fishermen blew foghorns there and citizens
turned out to watch sea warriors returning home.
Sailors stooped to kiss the earth.
Others scanned the crowded wharf for faces they might know.
The luckiest was welcomed by a woman who'd
journeyed up from Long Beach on the Union Pacific.
Sue watched the solemn greetings offered up
by ancient officers and municipal suits but
had no patience for their droning words.
She touched her husband's once familiar face:
toured that map of shrapnel scars and seared brown skin.
For now, she thought, *we've done enough.*
She took her husband by the arm
and with a look dismissed the waste and wanton lies of war,
promised rather highway enchantments and
jazz incantations, the sound of hopeless guitars
in a hundred Deep South honky-tonks.
Come on, said Sue. *Forget their flags.*
The open road is ours again and
every star that shines above it.
Let us go and pay them homage.
Let us pledge allegiance to ourselves.

Carnival

In the Key of G Major

Green is fading from the sweetgum leaves
Shadows getting longer under the eaves
Whole county's come down to see the fair
Whole county walking that courthouse square
They're selling fried corn dogs, mangos on a stick
Everybody's falling for them carnival tricks
Spend ten dollars for a two-dollar prize
Get it home before you realize

Everybody knows that it ain't no use
Walking around in them borrowed shoes
But the music starts and you can't refuse
The carnival's back in town

He's a black t-shirt with the sleeves cut out
She's fifteen now, she's got that little girl pout
Catches him looking at her standing there
Not sure what to do with that serious stare
They go riding on the Tilt-A-Whirl
Pistol-eyed boy and a halter-top girl
Get so dizzy that they have to hold hands
Walking underneath the rodeo stands

Everybody knows that it ain't no use
Searching for treasure without any clues
But the music starts and you can't refuse
The carnival's back in town.

Leaves go tumbling through the woods
And that ain't doing anybody good
It's like raindrops falling in a swimming pool
I don't want to be September's fool
I don't want to stand at the edge of town
Waiting for the wind to knock me down,
Waiting for the carnival to come around
Again…

There's a grown man over by the Ferris wheel
Thinking about how he used to feel
One day he won himself a shiny brass ring
Figured that it had to mean some damn thing
He gave it to a girl with hometown hair
She kissed him but she left him standing right there
She's a city girl now, a long time gone
I still remember her favorite song

(And it goes like this)

Everybody knows that it ain't no use
Looking for gold in a world full of blues
But the music starts and we can't refuse
The carnival's back in town…

REPEAT CHORUS

The All-Time Traveling Haiku All-Stars

Turns out heaven runs
350 to center, on
grass grown smooth as silk.

You can pick your squad
from the best that played the game.
I call dibs on these:

LF   *Ty Cobb*
Buy him his own bus.
His hook slides scarred third basemen.
Spit has more remorse.

3B   *Pete Rose*
Used humongous face
to knock down infield screamers.
Tough. (Could room with Cobb.)

CF   *Wille Mays*
As near perfect as
anyone sans wings can be.
He had magic bones.

RF   *Babe Ruth*
Cuchulain reborn.
Invented long-ball, made game
home for hero feats.

C   *Josh Gibson*
His shots never soared:
they cleared fences on a line,
telegraphic truths.

1B   *Lou Gehrig*
The gamer's gamer
savaged fast balls daily, for
almost fourteen years.

2B   *Rogers Hornsby*
His '24 mark
may be expansion-proof, the
horse-hide minded crank.

SS   *Ozzie Smith*
At short, he covered
more green earth than average
ice age. Hit some, too.

P   *Walter Johnson*
Idaho's phenom
threw faster than eyes could *see*.
Some elbows are blessed.

Power. Pitching. Speed.
Everything a great club needs.
With Ruth away from

nightclubs, whiskey, dames,
this nine could take on seraphs,
battle every frame—

barring rapture or
odd home field hops, might even
force a seventh game.

The Littlest Nazi

The littlest Nazi, Alice Green,
grew up with dreams inside her head
that girls like her were better girls
and other girls were better dead.

Not that she practiced violence:
most nights, she stuck to violin.
But she was not afraid to praise
the virtues of her snow-white skin.

It simply seemed to Alice Green
that fair complexions and blue eyes
implied a better sort of mind.
All else was dingy pious lies.

Small-minded people grew enraged,
and several chased her through the town,
while others filed civil suits
and tried to wear her family down

till one day Alice turned around
and quieted the ringing taunts.
All people ought to have the right
to speak and think the things they want,

said Alice Green. *This is my creed.*
We learn it every year in school,
and I do not wish to cause you harm
but I will NOT live by mob rule.

And so she stood and dared the crowd
to strike a slender nine-year-old
who'd simply tried to live her life
as best she heard what conscience told.

And not one there, of any hue,
could stand to smash that pretty face—
behind which worked a heart and mind
of just the same stuff as their race.

Said old Ben Levy, *Leave her be.*
She simply speaks as she believes.
We cannot make her love us all
or take her thoughts like palace thieves.

So Alice Green was given hugs
and all assembled made a vow
to let each other live in peace.
And so I will, she thought. *For now.*

A Beginner's Guide to Disappointment

1/Our Protagonist

Meet Bill Mattingly, a suburban kid
from Westlake's quiet, cedar-shaded streets.
You'd never catch these folks in hooded sheets
but if there's color here, it's been well hid.
Consider the promise in young Bill's looks:
a suitable specimen of the leading brand,
he's six feet tall, with hair like dirty sand
and eyesight blunted by too many books.
Our Bill grew up as lucky children do.
He watched TV, went to art-after-school,
spent hours in outfields and swimming pools.
When he earned his B.A. at age twenty-two,
the folks at the law school welcomed him in
as if they'd found some long-lost next of kin.

2/Law School

The ideal lawyer's not really the sort
you'd care to chat with at your local bar.
An *aficionado* of the way things are,
imagination is his last resort.
Our Bill would never be that perfect man.
It wasn't that he lacked the lawyer's mind,
more that he couldn't bear to waste his time
on daily coursework he could hardly stand.
A pronounced tendency to wander off—
to daydream through, *e.g.*, THE LEADING CASE—
combined in him with fear of losing face.
He read erratically, but just enough,
then bent his large head to almost his knees
to wrestle the Rule Against Perpetuities.

3/Bright Lights

Two years on, Bill lived Manhattan shoebox-style
in student digs near Columbia U.
(Illegally sublet. But what's that to you?)
Suffice it to say that it took him a while
to catalogue his strange new neighborhood:
Bodegas! Taxis! Street kids hawking crack!
He swore at first he'd catch the first flight back,
but Monday he showed up at Brown & Wood.
The firm took up three floors of One World Trade
and boasted panoramic harbor views.
Bill watched sailboats traverse the spangled blue,
tack east toward the cold Atlantic's fade.
They say those towers used to lean and sway
as if they were mainmasts. Bill decided to stay.

4/They Meet

In June a party, West 78th.
Sue wore jet black, motley of the thinking class,
and watched the room over her cocktail glass,
blunt-cut dark hair protecting an oval face.
She seemed much harder than the girls he'd known,
all attitude and unmasked arrogance,
and neither one saw sparks until they danced—
at first with other law school geeks, then alone.
She rolled her eyes at all his classic moves
(the Marvin Gaye Memorial Ecorgasm,
the Joseph K. Strummer Strafing Death Spasm)
as they drifted closer in the strobe-lit room.
At 4 a.m. they stumbled down Broadway.
Bill rode the train home from her place the next day.

5/Shared Interests

She was, he learned, a second-year at Penn:
hair black to almost blue, five-six, brown eyes.
Her Chinese name, *Chen Su*, Americanized,
became the less exotic "Susan Chen."
Like him, she was a law firm summer clerk.
They shared their histories a dozen times,
long mornings dissected the Sunday *Times*
and swapped tall tales about the egos at work.
As July weekends lingered, slow and sweet,
they seldom bothered to climb out of bed
and laughed at every idle word they said.
The world no longer seemed so incomplete.
In Texas, she said, he was bound to forget.
He told her not to give up on them yet.

6/What It Was, Sort Of

Consider the following hypotheses.
Bill wanted Sue because she seemed *apart*,
taboo, so different that it stirred his heart,
jump-starting certain dormant faculties,
among which possibly was gallantry,
a readiness to defend her from all harm
related to their walking arm-in-arm
in mostly unremarked miscegeny.
But then the opposite was also true.
Despite her Asian name and blue-black hair,
they found a hundred pointless things to share.
(She'd grown up watching "The Jeffersons" too.)
Or this: from that first night he heard her voice,
he never really felt he had a choice.

7/The First-Year

They wrote and telephoned—broke up—rejoined—
made then amended strict relationship rules,
and somehow through that last long year of school
they kept each other's distant hearts aligned.
That autumn, in a maze of parquet halls,
Bill Mattingly began to practice law.
He quickly lost his first-year's sense of awe:
the job was largely a series of conference calls.
Those days the Nikkei was a promised land,
America's collapse a lead-pipe cinch.
The firm billed time to giant Merrill Lynch,
and set out to sell the U.S. to Japan.
Call Bill a technician of currency flow,
an American servant of Sumitomo.

8/The Wedding

The church was suitably tweedy, and treed.
Sue's gown seemed stitched of saltwater pearl.
They both shed tears as the ceremony unfurled,
from procession to the Nicene Creed.
Even the reception went improbably well:
Suburban Texas, meet Pacific Rim.
The wildly mixed assemblage toasted them
with *gam bei!* and attempts at rebel yells.
All through that squid and roast duck feast
the couple took back every unkind word
they'd said, and some that neither one had heard.
They'd always have this to recall, at least:
a wedding done right, good friends at their side.
Bill kissed the cool hand of his whispering bride.

9/Full Schedules and Empty Containers

On Christmas Eve that year, Bill overpaid
some whiskered Canuck for his last gaunt fir
and lugged the tree uptown, a gift for her.
(She never asked him what the damn thing *weighed*.)
They schlepped to Greene Street and Lutece to eat,
indulged themselves in extravagant meals.
Why not? they said. This was why they did their deals,
worked till they could barely feel their tired feet.
Odd how so much can be justified when one
has drained his fourth glass of a fine Bordeaux.
They drank till restless waiters made them go,
then hurried home to beat the waking sun.
They prided themselves on their self-absorbed lives.
They barely had time to be husband and wife.

10/Hubris

Bill's Wall Street career lasted thirty-one months.
Not much by standard resume rules, but he
had spent too many Sunday nights buried
beneath prospectus texts in nine-point fonts.
Besides, ideas were bubbling in his brain:
Spenserian sagas! Clancy-like thrillers!
Tolkienesque epics with cauldron-born killers!
He left the firm to claim himself again,
surprised when no one tried to hold him back.
By late October he was working from home,
except for his laptop completely alone,
a wannabe Ginsberg or Kerouac.
Cut loose, he was finally free to write—
or founder in vast lineless seas of white.

11/Bohemia

At first it was only going to be a test:
a year to write the fictions he'd design
to edify that lumpy mass, mankind,
and earn some nifty royalty checks.
They piled a futon, books, and speakers so high
in their studio flat on the Upper West Side
it got damned hard to navigate inside
(they'd *in*hale to allow each other by).
The kitchen owned a view of Hudson blue.
From anywhere else it was roof collages,
10th Avenue, and parking garages.
They talked whenever they were able to.
Most nights she worked till 3:30 or 4,
a loyal grundoon of Cravath, Swaine & Moore.

12/The Divergence

For Sue, New York was all ability,
a place where former lives got sick and died.
Here no one cared you'd grown up ostracized,
Chinese amidst genteel hostility.
She loved the city's soups of race and creed
and felt most confident in milling groups.
Parade days, shopping, watching pick-up hoops
downtown seemed less pastime for her than *need*.
By contrast, Bill enjoyed a platitude
or two, and vistas of The Great Outdoors,
not least of all when panhandled by whores
and crackheads in their so-called neighborhood.
Thus soldiering on—Sue downtown, Bill at home—
they kept in intermittent touch by phone.

13/Blocked

Behold the scrivener, bent to his plot!
He paces, daydreams, types a paragraph,
takes time to brew himself a fresh carafe,
watches talk (Montel is hot; Ron Reagan's not).
Both eyes affixed on blockbuster sales,
he tries employing the new Russian Mob
to pull some mammoth inside trading job,
plows on for months with such ungainly tales.
The longer he works, the harder in his head
it seems to just admit the obvious:
his fiction isn't really worth the fuss.
He has a gift for turning gold to lead.
After several months of this, he tells a friend,
If only I had it to do over again.

14/Loose Ends

When do you know an effort's sure to fail?
When's wishing not enough to make it true?
No doubt they both desired to see it through,
to claim the glamorless secular grail
our marriages intend. I'm speaking of
a passion that may alter, but endure
through all the mundane years and furniture
to leave Esteem. Accord. Romantic love.
But Bill was no more what, for her, he'd been:
a prize in a natty Brooks Brothers suit,
her personal suburb—a substitute
for years when she was outside, looking in.
They grew ironic with each other's names.
Their fondest ambitions stopped sounding the same.

15/Another Attempt

His part-time coaching job was better called
Pre-Teenage Babysitting in Full Sweats.
He walked his first- and third-grade athletes out
to Central Park to torture soccer balls,
to learn profanity and corner kicks.
It wasn't exactly heroic stuff.
He never thought he was *instructing* enough.
He did find, though, that he enjoyed this mix
of parenting, omnipotence, and play.
Next autumn he was given a fifth-grade class
for keeps—for good—from math to weekly mass,
and found himself teaching nine hours a day.
His worst weeks still seemed only minutes long.
That April, Sue was assigned to Hong Kong.

16/Hong Kong

Although she promised she'd meet him at Kai Tak,
Sue didn't show. Bill found the taxi queue,
gave a driver named Mung a map marked in blue,
leaned back till he sat in front of her flat.
She lived on the island, at the Royal Court,
and welcomed him with marked hesitation,
announcing a sort of in-house separation,
a joint tenancy of the last resort.
Bill's job, she said, was obtaining a *job*—
not writing, not teaching, but actual work,
the kind that paid money and dependable perks;
she'd no longer fund a cash-challenged slob.
Sue traveled first-class to Saigon and Dubai.
Bill watched young prostitutes dance in Wanchai.

17/That Trip to China

A week's trip through Guangdong: he went by train
alone from Sung Wan to half-built Shenzhen,
stopped there for passport scrutiny, then
resumed the tour, northbound through sun again.
It proved extremely hard to look someplace
and not see several someones looking back.
The train was packed. On two adjacent tracks,
an army of the local populace
was toting, lifting, and hammering steel rails.
In brown Guangzhou the earth seemed ill at ease.
Bill strolled through streets of unamused Chinese,
priced Qing Ping Market's suckling cats for sale.
No need to say what the snake blood was for:
we all suspect we're capable of more.

18/The Drinking Life

Even amidst Hong Kong's hectic advance,
bright pockets still survived. Green Mai Po Marsh.
Kadoorie Farm. Lone kite cries—keening, harsh—
above the city's teeming anthill dance.
Bill's mass-mailed resumes brought few replies.
He picked up PR work, paid by the hour,
and wrote catalogue copy in office towers
beatifying Swedish merchandise.
By December he realized he was looking less.
He wandered the trails up Victoria Peak,
stayed solidly drunk for almost a week,
re-met his wife over her pond-sized desk.
There he found out what others already knew.
Sue was just doing what she had to do.

19/Gone to Texas

The entire flight home from Hong Kong, he slept.
Then Austin: the Hell Where Everyone Drives.
That night, stuck in traffic on I-35,
he placed his head on the wheel and he wept.
For several months he was parallel men:
one living present tense, one right beside
in some impossible world still with his bride
and screwing things up all over again.
He'd think of Sue while he was driving home
or leaving home, speak to her *sotto voce*.
All day and night was when he missed her most;
three times he killed uncaring telephones.
That March it rained, non-stop, for a week.
Sometimes he felt too desperate to speak.

20/The End

Eight months later, he gets the divorce.
The world is gray, maybe fifty degrees,
not a single leaf to be found on the trees—
a stone tableau of his own bland remorse.
Through armored doors and the x-ray machine,
Bill makes his way to Judge Covington's court:
today she'll preside over those of his sort.
He's worried mostly that he'll cause a scene.
The judge asks questions. Who knows what they are?
His last several answers are meaningless sounds.
The court reporter, embarrassed, looks down,
as Judge Covington offers to call him a car.
There's really no way to soft-pedal the case
or to wish himself anywhere else but this place.

21/Basketball

Live oak roots crack sidewalks over their knees.
He stops, looks up, thinks he sees her in cars,
but does not. He walks the neighborhood for hours
until he's numbed himself again, nearly
nothing in his head but the smell of old exhaust.
Basketball players pirouette as he passes.
No one else seems to see how the sun sears the grass,
or cares to see. And he tries to stay lost,
but buses run. Children laugh, and fall, and yawn.
The brick walls around him are thick with spray paint.
Bright calendars advertise beer and dead saints.
He numbered his days by her. Now she's gone.
Straight streets seem to swim in the heat. He persists.
Says still, there is this. What he felt. He insists.

22/Discretion

Meet William Mattingly. He'll shake your hand,
incline his head, converse attentively.
He's known around these offices to be
a decent guy, not hard to understand.
Inside his head, though, he's a random disaster,
a burning car by the side of the road,
a discarded toaster, a never-kissed toad.
He wonders why he's not aging faster.
He still keeps, in his desk, a framed picture
from the first few days they spent in New York
and even now it pulls him from his work
and even now, some nights, he dreams of her.
But these are things Bill Mattingly won't tell.
Some stories simply do not end so well.

Foot Soldiers

A clammy day in March we
lifted off from Bergstrom Airport, each of us
carrying our own soft cargo of flesh and lactic acid
like an emissary from our ancestors. The flight was mostly men.
We wore suits from Dillard's. Six-pound shoes.
Off to tend to summary judgment motions and
small-group insurance plans, we kept ourselves inside ourselves
till the plane fell through some sky trap door and
cans of tomato juice rolled for the exits. It got rougher, too.
We spent those seven minutes of mortality trying not to stare at
each other, not even to speak—just to wear our random sentences with dignity,
like a kind of instant tumor. All the time I wanted to shout,
Does anyone else realize we're miles above the nearest freeway?
That if this air won't act its age they'll have to call experts
     to figure out who we were?
That we're turbines away from a gymnasium floor,
with numbers tied to what were our toes?
What is God thinking? Are we all just parts of a larger brain?
Will I be forgiven? Who makes mud? Can I hug you?
till the atmosphere unclenched and everyone
began to look around. I even saw uncertain smiles
before the whole gray group returned again to spreadsheets,
to blueprints, grant forms, and secured transactions.
All matters of the greatest urgency, of course, and by the time we reached
Hobby I had almost forgotten this brief experiment in communal dread.
I stepped out into the rain, smelled cigarettes and oil
and hustled to grab the nearest cab.
I was beaten by a fellow near-death pilgrim who said
Sorry, pal. I got here first and
shut the goddamned door.

Baz

Her Arab colt is
Baz, which means
the wild horse of Yemen.
But not yet.
Three months on
we still stop every night
to watch as he
blinks heavily,
drowsy, soft-faced as
a thicket-hidden
fawn.

Cedar shavings
cling to him
like sleep.
Stay down, she says.
He cocks one hoof.

Walking back
through stars as
thick as snow I hear
a rabbit run
a mile away. I breathe
to break my lungs and she
says all of this
is ours.

www.ingramcontent.com/pod-product-compliance
Lightning Source LLC
Chambersburg PA
CBHW020514030426
42337CB00011B/383